The

IDENTITY MANUAL

How To Define Your True Identity, Escape The Identity Crisis & Find Fulfillment

FRANKLIN H. EZENWA

ISBN 978-1-7752543-3-1 Paperback
978-1-7752543-4-8 Ebook

MOTIVATE AND INSPIRE OTHERS!

"Share This Book"

Retail $20.99

Special Quantity

30 - 49 Books	$18.99
50 - 99 Books	$16.99
100 - 499 Books	$13.99
500 - 999 Books	$10.99
1,000+ Books	$8.99

To Place an Order Contact:

Franklin H. Ezenwa

franklin@allroundachievers.com

https://allroundachievers.com

THE IDEAL PROFESSIONAL SPEAKER FOR YOUR NEXT EVENT!

Any organization that wants to inspire and develop their people to become "extraordinary", needs to hire Franklin for a keynote and/or workshop training!

TO CONTACT OR BOOK FRANKLIN TO SPEAK:

Franklin H. Ezenwa

franklin@allroundachievers.com

https://allroundachievers.com

THE IDEAL COACH FOR YOU!

If you're ready to overcome challenges, have major breakthroughs and achieve higher levels, then you will love having Franklin as your coach!

TO CONTACT FRANKLIN:

Franklin H. Ezenwa

franklin@allroundachievers.com

https://allroundachievers.com

DEDICATION

I dedicate this book to my lovely family, my close friends, my mentors, coaches and to everyone else who has contributed to making me the person that I am. Thank you for encouraging, challenging, inspiring, supporting and loving me. Also, to God for being my everything.

TABLE OF CONTENTS

Introduction

A message to you

"The strongest force in the universe is a human being living consistently with his identity; that is the need to stay consistent in how we define ourselves." - Tony Robbins

Quick question to ask yourself: "Who am I?" Yes! Who are you?

- Are you your job/career title? (e.g. a Registered Nurse, a Doctor, a Football player, a Janitor, a Mechanic, etc)

- Are you your role in your home? (e.g. a Wife, a Son, a Father, a Daughter, etc)

- Are you your accomplishments? (e.g. 10X #1 Bestselling Author, First Female CEO at XYZ company, #1 Top Student of the Year, Best Employee of Year, Best Boring Comedian on the century, etc)

- Are you your failures? (e.g. the one who failed launching 3 businesses in 3 years, the one who messed up multiple musicals performance, the one who missed sales targets each quarter, etc)
- Are you your possessions? (e.g. your million-dollar rental properties portfolio, your papers in the bank, your flashy car(s), your big house with a swimming pool, your businesses, etc)
- Are you the likes, comments and views on your social media posts?

Looking at the option(s) you picked, now imagine that you were stripped of all that you had selected from the list above i.e. accomplishment, possessions, etc . Ask yourself the same question again - "Who Am I?" Are you still the same person, or are you now a "nobody"? If you're still the same person, good for you! If you answered otherwise, just stay with me here and know that you're not alone.

Maybe this is your first time thinking deeply about that question. Honestly speaking, irrespective of what your answer was, I am very glad you got to, at least, think about that question. Why? First off, that is a question of identity, and, I believe, that it is one of the most fundamental questions we can ask ourselves. The reason being that your response to that question determines how you see yourselves, the world and the people around you, and consequently, how the world will respond to you. In short, let's just say it will determine the course of your life.

You may have read stories of great sports players, celebrities or executives of highly prestigious firms who, after their career abruptly ended due to an injury or unexpected hardship, found themselves lost in a dark, lonely space. They basically didn't know who they were anymore because the one thing that they had tied their identity to and told themselves they were had now been taken away from them. Sadly, as a result of that, a number of them plunged into severe depression and in the worst cases, some ended their lives.

Besides that, your identity determines your behavior. Consciously or subconsciously, you tend to act/behave in a manner that is consistent with who you believe you are. For example, if you tell yourself that you're a shy person, you're less likely to be the one at a social gathering going around to introduce yourself to other people. Similarly, if you tell yourself that you're a failure, you may never make attempts to succeed at something. And even if you do, you'll always find a way to subconsciously self-sabotage, so you can stay true to who you said you are. And, of course, there are a gazillion more reasons why this is one of the most fundamental questions we can ask ourselves; but I'll just park it all here .

Something's got to change right now

"I can't continue like this any more. Whatever it takes, God, I am ready for a change..." There I was in my bedroom, talking to God somewhat in surrender, which had been a big challenge for me. I was just fed up. I had been struggling with a serious, severe issue with my identity and at that time, I had hit a rock bottom experience in my life. If there was ever a time I felt the most confused about who I was, it was at that period.

Coupled with the loss of senses of self, purpose and control, I had also felt very miserable, as I was plagued with incessant anxiety and panic attacks - not to talk about my relationship with fear (hello fear!). Fear had paralyzed me: fear of the unknown; the fear that I wouldn't get what I wanted; the fear that I would lose what I had; along with other negative, pessimistic thought patterns that got me petrified. Living in fear caused me to create this bubble of self-centeredness that, as you would imagine, negatively impacted many of my close relationships at the time.

Part of this awful experience also stemmed from the fact that I was stuck in the comparison trap, trying to match up with some moving standard which I always never seemed to hit - no matter how hard I tried. Oh, did I mention that I was already sick and tired of the shiny object syndrome? I was almost always on a quest, trying to find the next 'big thing' or as some would say, my acres of diamond. I thought the thing that was missing was out there somewhere. So, I jumped from place to place but to no avail. And because I didn't know who I was, I had a hard time figuring out what I was here to do, which was why I was struggling to identify what path to take.

For as long as I can remember, this persisted for quite some time; but I tried to wade through while enduring, hoping things would get better by chance, you know! It became clear to me that there was a problem somewhere. That was when I decided to just surrender, become vulnerable and get some help. And you know what? I'm glad I did. (Do you relate to any of these? Perhaps it's time to get help.)

"Do not let the roles you play in life make you forget who you are." — Roy T. Bennett

Why this book was written

Someone once said that we live life forward but we understand it backward. In other words, we can only connect the dots looking backwards. I didn't realize that I was going through what is known as an identity crisis until much later after I had escaped that awful period (scary eh?). I had heard about that term before, but interestingly while I was in it, I was oblivious to that fact. While in that black hole, one thing I remembered was saying to myself and telling God was that after I got out of that awful place, I would help as many people as possible to do the same. And this book is part of my attempt to do just that. I really wanted to give a good account of that journey going from being lost, miserable and frustrated to where I am now with much more clarity about my identity and purpose. It was for this reason that I documented most of the key lessons I learnt from different sources including the exercises I had to do. (I hope you also get to take those exercises, if needed.) This experience taught me a very crucial lesson: taking action is where transformation comes.

Apart from that, in the last couple of years, there has been a significant jump in the use of the internet and social media which have their own good and bad sides. But as you may already know, social media can do a lot of damage to you if not put to check. In fact, there are studies [1] that show how social media negatively impacts individuals with different outcomes (e.g. anxiety, depression, unhealthy comparison and envy towards people, etc). I've tasted the dark side of social media and know stories of folks who have as well. One thing I can say is that, we're more susceptible to the negative device of social media mostly when we're struggling with an identity issue (this encompasses issues with self-esteem, self-image, etc which are all covered in this book). This is an area I feel very passionate about, like it's a calling of mine to help people get clear on their identity so they can be the best version of themselves and live the amazing life they're created for. I want that for you!

Who this book is for

Irrespective of your age, role, status, etc, if you're struggling with your identity- i.e. not knowing who you are and why you're on earth - I believe you'll find a lot of gems in this book to help you get clarity on those areas. Also, if you think that you or someone you know is walking the street of Identity Crisis, then surely this book is for you. In addition, if you find yourself caught up in the comparison trap, envying other people because you feel you're not as gifted or talented as they are, and wishing you could possess their gifts because you feel you don't have any at all, then this book is definitely for you. In short, this book will help you to know, love and accept yourself, and guide you towards unleashing your potential so that you can live a fulfilling life.

How to make the most of this book

There's one thing I strongly believe in now more than ever before and that is - taking action. When we do nothing, nothing happens - no matter what we're hoping for or expecting. Ever since learning this lesson, I've become very intentional about applying the knowledge I glean. I hope you buy my sentiment with this too.

I wouldn't want you to just browse through this book and say to yourself how cool it was (I hope you would say it's cool though!) and let things end there. It's my hope that as you go through it, you'll take the time to pick up one or more salient points that you can apply to make a change to your life where needed. To help with that, I've outlined exercises at the end of each chapter which I would encourage you to attempt. This is how you experience the power of transformation. The kind that comes from taking action on what you know because knowledge on its own is only potential power; it becomes power only when you act on it.

With that being said, if you're ready to start out on this journey of fulfillment to knowing, accepting and loving yourself so you can become all that you were created to be, then I will catch up with you in the next chapter.

*To get **FREE** bonus resources (which includes a copy of the workbook for this book), be sure to visit rebrand.ly/FreeGiftIdentity. (You'll also* *be notified when my upcoming course on Identity launches.)*

17

be notified when my upcoming course on Identity launches.)

Chapter 1

Define your own true identity

"Identity cannot be found or fabricated but emerges from within when one has the courage to let go. " - Doug Cooper

Imagine someone who doesn't know you closely trying to tell you who you are. It's like me trying to convince you that you're not the person represented on your driver's license or on your international passport or other piece of identification. That would be ridiculous, I know.

Likewise, when it comes to your identity, i.e. who you believe and know you are, how absurd it is to let the world, that doesn't know you, define who you are? Your pieces of identification reveal some aspects of who you are, e.g. your name, age, nationality, etc. Some of the data was passed on to you by your parents who know and love you so closely. Hopefully you concur with the data and that's why you could have them added to your identification which you boldly showcase to the world. Beyond those inherited data, there is still a lot more data that you were innately created with, which are obviously different from your parents, and define you in a unique and special way. That's what's interesting to dig into.

So what exactly is identity?

According to the Merriam-Webster's dictionary, identity refers to the qualities, beliefs, character, personality that makes a person different from others. To supplement that, the Oxford dictionary says that identity denotes the characteristics, feelings or beliefs that make people different from others. (Read those lines again till they sink in.) I can't explain how much I love and agree with the choice of words in those definitions. (Merriam-Webster; Oxford; you guys are just so awesome!)

First off, notice how the elements in the definitions have nothing to do with external things (e.g. the money in the bank, accolades, possessions, roles, etc). In other words, identity isn't tied to things or labels; it's the inner core of who you are. So, when did you come to believe that external things define you?

Second, identity is unique. That's what distinguishes you from people with whom you may even share similar or same beliefs or attributes, even your family members. If identity is what makes you uniquely lovely and amazing, why then would you ever wish to be someone else? That's like choosing to discard the original version of a precious being to go pick up a copy version of a different being. Last time I checked, the world doesn't appreciate copy versions more than the original. And I am one hundred percent certain that you don't either.

That said, identity is who you are at your core. It's what makes you uniquely 'You'. No one else, apart from your Creator, knows you more than you know yourself. Going by that, it simply means that no one else is qualified enough to define you. You alone have the right, power and choice to define 'You' based on how the Creator masterfully and beautifully made you. Is this all making sense to you?

"You are here with a unique purpose. Stop letting others define you. Stop letting others dilute you. Don't be bullied or pressured into being less than you are." - Steve Maraboli

Why it's important to define your own identity

Knowing what you know now about identity, isn't it sad to think that you can look to the outside world, that has no clue about you, to define who you are and what you should become? It definitely is, if you ask me.

I remember falling for this trap and living in that way for a very long time. At that time, I was seeking the world's stamp of validation over who I am and what I was put on earth to do with my life. The experience was misery; the thought of it alone makes me sick, and I wouldn't wish that for anyone. I didn't have clarity on who I was, and instead of looking within, I searched the outside world. This led me to wishing to become like certain people whom I had admired. Also, I was striving to reach certain moving standards of success in the world's eyes. And when it was becoming increasingly difficult to hit these, I felt frustrated and discontent with where I was. This was just an endless cycle.

A huge part of the frustration I had experienced stemmed from the fact that the approach I was following didn't fit well with my core. I was trying to become a copy of someone else and was pursuing certain moving standards, some of which violated the core of who I am - my identity. It's like trying to fit a square block into a triangular opening. That just won't fit. Don't get me wrong, it's not bad to admire others or to observe certain standards. It only becomes a problem when it causes a problem with you trying to become someone or something you're not which opposes and disposes of your true self and identity.

When you look to the outside world to determine your identity and to tell who you're to become, chances are that it will point you in the opposite direction. And that to me is a disaster.

"Be who you are and say what you feel because those who mind don't matter and those who matter don't mind." - Dr. Seuss

How to build your identity

By this time I hope you can already see the danger of permitting other people to tell you who you are and what you should become. This is for the obvious reason that they don't have the 'blueprint' of your life like you and the Creator do. So, how then do you determine or define your true identity?

In the course of deciding to intentionally define my identity, there were a number of practices I had to do which I had gleaned from different sources. They really helped me a lot in figuring out the identity thing. I've encapsulated them into 5 key points. You're welcome to try them out. Feel free to stick to what works and discard what doesn't. Here comes:

1. Identify your beliefs and labels

You are bound within the corners of your beliefs. What you believe to be true affects who you are and who you choose to become. Most of your beliefs originate from what people may have said to you or about you - whether positive or negative. Someone may have called you names or labeled you as something that didn't sit well with you. But maybe at some point you stopped fighting it and just accepted it as your fate. I'm here to let you know that no human determines your fate and destiny but you. So, it's about time to drop every label and belief that doesn't resonate with who you are at your core. Every limiting belief and label has to make way for you to live your true identity.

2. Learn more about your wonderful self

This includes your personality, passions, purpose, interests, gifts, talents, special abilities, strengths, weaknesses, values, etc. I thought I knew 'Me' well enough until I started out on this exercise only to get blown away by how little I knew about myself. Go ahead and give it a shot - you may just be blown away too. More on this in the next chapter.

3. Accept what your Creator/Higher power says about you

Depending on your beliefs, you may identify with a Higher Power who you believe created you for a purpose. Just as a manufacturer fully knows the features, capability and purpose for what he's created, I believe the same applies with you and your Higher Power/Creator. And so it behooves you to know and to embrace what your Creator says about you and to run with it because not only is it true, it could just be the best. As a person of faith, I believe in God; that He created me and says many beautiful and powerful things about me, and that He's got a wonderful plan and purpose for my life beyond my imaginations. What He says about me is constant and trumps what anyone else says or thinks about me. It's in Him that the foundation of my identity lives. How about you?

4. Find the right role models

In the course of figuring out who you are and who you want to become, since you haven't done that before, there's a tendency to get stuck and lost in this rut. This is where having the right role models comes in. People who will inspire you to dream bigger; people who will boost your confidence in the possibility of your dream becoming a reality; people who will nudge you to say, "if he/she can do it, then I can do it too." ; people you deeply connect with, whose inner fire stir up your flame. Obviously, the goal here is not for you to become a copy of them, but to learn from them, get inspired and motivated by them, so that you can solidify your identity.

5. Reconcile with your past

Although you're products of your past, you mustn't let your past define your present and future. It can be tough thinking about some of the behaviors and actions of yours in the past and feeling that it's just who you are and that you're stuck with that. You know, I remember feeling that way at some point in my life, especially about how sometimes I had acted unlovingly towards others and even hurt some people around me. I held this against myself for a while and it was really a big struggle letting go. Obviously, I had to admit my mistakes, make amends where I could, and turn a new leaf, as this wasn't serving me well.

Eventually, I learnt to give myself the gift of grace and forgiveness and completely dropped it all off. I am so glad I don't have to pull my past into my future (phew!). So my friend, give yourself permission to be kind to yourself; give yourself grace and forgiveness; right the wrongs; turn a new leaf and move on . You're not what you did or who you were in the past (assuming you've turned a new leaf).

It takes time to define and build our identity to make it align with our core, if that's not where it's at already. What's important is that we can clearly define what that ideal state is and then walk consistently towards it; and once we're there, to ensure that we remain right there as we live it out each day unapologetically. It takes courage to do that, but I believe it's worth the effort because doing that alone brings freedom - freedom to be who we've been created to be and not be sorry about it. I believe everyone loves to experience this.

Do you know how it feels to have a treasure trove of precious gems and not even know it? You've been endowed with seeds of greatness, unique combination of gifts, talents and special abilities; but there's a problem. Not everyone takes the time to deliberately find out what's in the treasure trove.

In the next chapter, I'll walk you through how you can begin to discover more about what makes you who you are and how you can leverage those to become who you're meant to be and, hence, strengthen your identity. This will definitely lead to a transformation in your life. I just can't wait. So, what are you waiting for? Flip it! (Oh, don't forget to do the action exercise first!)

Action exercises

1. What labels or beliefs have you allowed to define who you are? Which of those do you need to drop off

now?

2. What does your Higher Power/Creator say about who you are and what your purpose is? How can you begin living by those daily?

3. Identify 1-3 role models who you resonate with in different areas of life. How do they inspire and motivate you? What can you learn from them to apply to your life without tending to become a copy version of them ?

4. Is there anything from your past that's blocking you from becoming the person you want to be? What do you need to do today to let go of that unsettled past?

Chapter 2

Get on the self-discovery journey

"The greatest discovery in life is self-discovery. Until you find yourself you will always be someone else. Become yourself." —
Myles Munroe

Have you ever caught yourself wishing and praying that you had certain gifts and talents just like someone you admire? In fact, you fixated on it to the extent that you accused the Creator of being unfair for making that person more gifted and talented than yourself. Not just that, you even felt like you weren't given any talents or gifts and so you just had to copy someone else. Do you relate to any of that?

Do I even have gifts, talents and special abilities like others?

Ok, let me just break the ice and say that the entire picture I just painted above used to be my story at some point. Honestly, there was a time in my life when I felt I wasn't given any gifts, talents and special abilities. I had a number of people out there who I admired so much. They were like superstars, doing big things with their gifts, talents and special abilities. Since I felt that I had zero gifts and talents, I thought that the smart thing to do was to imitate others so, at least, I could do something with my life. You know! You can imagine how that panned out without me telling you - which I don't think you want to know exactly - but to give you a hint: it was disastrous!

I didn't know how all of the identity thing worked back then, but it was miserable trying to become a copy of others. I had just set an impossible target for myself. Each time I noticed how far away I was from hitting the goal in spite of my sweat, tears and effort, I would get frustrated, sad, mad and bad. And now, the same people I was admiring became my target for envy because seemingly, they had given me an unattainable moving target to pursue, which was causing me a lot of anguish. That's exactly what happens when you have a moving target for a goal you can't control and, should I say, one that you probably aren't meant to be aiming for, because it only leads to a frustrating spiral.

Oh, did I mention that I was also in a beef with God? I felt like He had just made me an empty barrel without any gifts, talents and special abilities, a far cry from those other folks I so admired. And there I was, trying to fix the broken, incomplete thing He had created. Poor me! So I thought. All of these continued for a while, until things began to change and I started realizing how wrong I had been about the whole thing.

"When I discover who I am, I'll be free." — *Ralph Ellison, Invisible Man*

Everyone has gifts, talents, and special abilities (you included, of course)

As I began learning more about God's love and fairness towards all of His creations along with inspiring, back stories of some of those individuals I admire, I was beginning to see that everyone was created equally with gifts, talents, special abilities and superpowers. You may be asking - *"why then does it always seem like some have while the rest don't?"* That's a great question and I'm glad you thought about it. Well, the answer lies in **self-discovery**.

One thing I found is that those folks whom I admired literally spent time discovering, unleashing and developing their gifts, talents and abilities. Many of them started with not knowing about themselves to mastering themselves, and becoming the superstars that they are today (It always helps to look at the full picture.) I would imagine that the same is true about those folks you admire as well.

Upon realizing this, my eyes opened; the light bulbs turned on; the heavens rejoiced. I knew exactly what I was missing and so I set out immediately to get on that journey to discover, unleash and develop my gifts, talents, and special abilities. Maybe one day, I thought to myself, I would be a superstar like those other superstars that I admire, and join forces with them to do great things in the world. And what does this mean for you? It means that, irrespective of what you may think or have been told, you've been endowed with seeds of greatness, gifts, talents and special abilities just waiting to be discovered and unleashed.

The topic of self-discovery isn't taught at schools (at least not the ones I attended and know) and somehow, we all have to learn about it ourselves. Sincerely, I'm very happy that I got to know about it when I did, even though earlier would have been better. It has radically transformed my life and I hope it does the same for you. Before jumping into the self-discovery process, I would like to whet your appetite a bit by sharing why I believe that it is essential for everyone.

So why care to embark on the self-discovery journey?

I am sure there are possibly a gazillion benefits for getting on the self-discovery journey, but permit me to share few which I think you'll really appreciate:

1. **Dwarfs inferiority complex and boosts confidence**

Have you ever felt the smack of an inferiority complex? If yes, then I guess it was because you encountered someone who exhibited a certain quality or demeanor and you felt you had nothing like that or nothing at all. What if at that moment you reminded yourself that you actually had remarkable qualities and strengths. How different would that make you feel? Powerful, right? Knowing about your strengths keeps you away from the snare of feeling inferior and hence, boosts confidence because you know that you've got something special and unique just like everyone else.

2. **Increases Emotional Intelligence (self-awareness, specifically)**

Upon embarking on the self-discovery journey, not only did I become more aware of myself; I also noticed that my awareness for people rose as well. I was beginning to see and focus more on what makes others unique, special, human and worth appreciating. Prior to that, I am ashamed to say that I was usually very quick to find fault in others so I could criticize them inwardly or verbally. I was merely projecting on others what I didn't like about myself. But ever since practicing self-awareness (which is a core component of Emotional Intelligence (E.I)), I have experienced a significant difference. Studies have identified different qualities that most successful people have, and there's this one quality that showed up, can you guess what it is? It is self-awareness.

3. **Keeps one away from the comparison trap**

One salient lesson that the self-discovery journey has taught me is that everyone is special, unique and different; hence, your journey in life can't be the exact same as someone else's. This showed me that it is not wise to envy others; wish to be someone else just for their gifts/talents sake, or dump my gifts and strengths to aggressively pursue someone else's. This reminds me of the time when I was beginning my speaking career. I would try to imitate and compare myself with other veteran speakers because I thought I had no gift/talent in that area. And that didn't go well at all. I eventually learnt this truth - we've been blessed with peculiar gifts, talents and special abilities, so why envy someone else's?

What that means for you is that if you decide to be a copy of someone else, who's going to become the original that you were created to be? No one! And then your life would be gone with no trace in the sand of time, because you were only a shadow of some superstar - meanwhile you were also a superstar, but never gave your light permission to shine. That's why I couldn't agree any more with Ralph Waldo Emerson when he said, *"Envy is ignorance and imitation is suicide"* .

4. **Gives you insight into your life's purpose**

Knowing who you are can literally help you come to understand why you were put here on earth. That is because functions/features point to purpose. For example, when you see the wings of an airplane or the rotor blades of a helicopter, you instantly know that they were built to fly. Same way you observe the shape of a sports car or a ship and you know exactly why they were designed that way. In the same vein, when you discover who you are, what makes you unique and special (i.e. your features, gifts, etc), that can open you up to the world of your purpose.

5. **Leads to fulfillment**

Mark Twain once remarked, *"The two most important days in your life are the day you are born and the day you find out why."* I concur with that completely. There's nothing as fulfilling as living each day knowing confidently who you are and why you were put on earth while living out your purpose. In short, living life without a purpose is meaningless; but life with purpose brings fulfillment.

Surely, the list can go on and on but I think this should do - for now.

" 'Know thyself' was written over the portal of the antique world. Over the portal of the new world, 'Be thyself' shall be written." ~ Oscar Wilde

Elements of self-discovery

Hopefully, by now you see how invaluable the self-discovery journey is, and can't wait to see what's next.

I want to begin this by making it clear that what I am about to share here is based on my own self-discovery journey. Different people may have their own different journeys and experiences, and may even have a fancy name for it; but this was what raised my awareness and hence transformed my life - literally. Permit me to also state that this is a journey that no one else can take for you because we all have a different path in life. That said, I am more than glad to share with you what I have learnt since embarking on this life-changing self-discovery journey. Here they are in no particular order:

Checking in with self regularly

At any given instant, do you know why you feel the way you do? It's mostly because your thoughts are sending some signals to your brain and that gets you to feel a certain way and consequently act out in accordance with the thought pattern. For example, if you're feeling fearful at a point, it's because you have fearful thoughts parading your mind and possibly trying to paralyze you. Most times, this thought-feeling flow never gets explored, even though it can tell a lot about our internal state and uncover patterns that need to be worked on. This is where self-awareness comes into the picture: being conscious of what you're thinking about and how that makes you feel.

I remember a time in my life where I was almost constantly battling with intense anxiety and panic attacks. It got so severe that I would experience tightness in my chest, being paranoid, while in a very low and dismal mood. This went on for so long that I actually thought it was normal, and so, I never confronted it to find out what exactly was going wrong. I had accepted this negative pattern that was silently eating me up.

Later on, I learnt from different sources, including coaches I had worked with, that my feelings stemmed from my thoughts. I was then given an exercise to check in with myself regularly. As part of the checking-in exercise, whenever I felt anxious or fearful at any point, I would ask myself what I was thinking about, and then confront it.

After doing this exercise for a couple of days, it wasn't hard to see that I had been swimming in an ocean of destructive, negative thought patterns. The negative thoughts themselves were coming from horrible beliefs that I had been nursing at the time, all of which were driven by fear. Each time I felt negative emotions, I would literally pause to ask myself what I was thinking while I placed one of my hands over my chest. With that I would challenge the negative thoughts and the belief behind the thoughts till I disarmed them in that moment. Whenever I did this, along with some breathing exercise, I could feel the negative, toxic energy escape my pressure-tightened chest, and I would feel light and calm again until the next anxiety attack. I did this continuously until I finally identified a number of the beliefs that were keeping me stuck in this negative, anxious and fearful cycle. Gladly, I was able to tackle those beliefs head on - thanks to the power of self-awareness practiced in this manner. I still practice this technique till date, even though I don't battle with negative thoughts to the degree that I did back then.

The bottomline here for you is that practicing self-awareness can be a great way to uncover certain limiting beliefs that are not serving you which you may want to consider dropping off. This checking-in practice helped me to change my state/mood which later resulted in me changing the story (i.e. belief) I told myself in certain areas where I was limiting myself. This is very important because as studies have shown that of the thousands of thoughts we think everyday, about 85% of them are negative (yes, a whopping 85%). In fact, they dubbed this Automatic Negative Thoughts - ANT for short which is the default mode. What's even more scary is that about 95% of our thoughts are repeated. In other words, we tend to think about the same things every day. That's why you really want to be very intentional about what you're thinking because what you think, you will feel and experience. And the quality of your life, to a huge degree, is determined by the quality of your emotions like Tony Robbins says.

Although I have shared how I applied this technique in identifying negative emotions/ beliefs, I believe the same can be used for the positive ones too (i.e. recognizing the empowering beliefs so you can stick with them). What's worth remembering is that your feelings/emotions are triggered by your thoughts, which in turn are birthed by your beliefs.

Dig deep into your personality

Have you ever done any personality tests? I found them very handy when learning more about myself. I remember having to do a number of them including the 16Personalities/ Myer Briggs and Color Code personality tests. Not only did the tests reveal very interesting qualities about me, they also explained why I exhibited certain behaviors. And because I knew why I behaved in a certain way, I realized that I wasn't some weird alien, and decided to be more kind and understanding towards myself.

For example, according to the Color Code, I am predominantly Red-Blue which is dynamic; (by the way, the other two colors in that paradigm are White and Yellow). The Red folks are characterized by being power/control-freaks, vision-focused, action-oriented, harsh, domineering, entrepreneurial, etc. And some of the features of Blue folks include being self-disciplined, quality-obsessed, fulfilled especially by helping others, self-judgmental, insecure, self-righteous, etc. Interestingly, the descriptions of both codes almost perfectly matched my behaviors at the time to a very very large extent (I continue to work on the weaknesses both codes have, though). But honestly, I was amazed by how accurate the test was in depicting my personality snapshot. In fact, I remember working with a coach at the time who went further to break things down to explain why, for example, I would overthink decisions, get very hard on and critical of myself, feel very insecure, easily point out faults, etc. I've gotten some people to do these tests and they were equally amazed by the accuracy of the results. (You should consider doing them as well; the results may blow your mind away as well.)

Knowing all of these really opened my eyes even more to the person I had been operating as on auto-pilot. And, of course, I had to work on myself thoroughly to eliminate those weaknesses/negative aspects of the personality types so I could not only relate better to myself but to others as well. Funny enough, with my knowledge of these personality tests, sometimes, whenever I am interacting with someone even at speaking gigs, my mind tries to detect what category they fall into on one of those personality tests. This helps me to meet and relate with people where they are. In a number of cases, the predictions are accurate and the person is surprised how I was able to explain certain behaviors they normally exhibit, even without them having told me.(It makes me feel like a magician sometimes.)

I must say this though; I believe that personality tests only reveal a snapshot of who you are operating as at that point in time. In other words, personality isn't completely permanent in the sense that we can change the behaviors we don't like and further reinforce those that serve us using conditioning. In fact, there's an amazing book, "*Personality Isn't Permanent: Break Free from Self-Limiting Beliefs and Rewrite Your Story*" by Dr. Benjamin Hardy, which emphasizes the fact that we can update our personality, especially addressing those parts that don't serve us right.

Nonetheless, taking a deeper dive into your personality definitely helps to raise self-awareness.

"Work on your strengths until your weaknesses become irrelevant" ~ John C. Maxwell

Discovering strengths, gifts and talents

"Work on your weakness! Work on your weakness!!" I bet you've heard those words countless times, and may

even have been instructed to do just that. It's been in the air for ages. How many times, though, have you been instructed to identify and develop your strengths? Almost rarely, I would suppose. And that was why, for a long time, I had focused so much on my weaknesses that I wasn't conscious of my strengths. My life changed the moment I became more aware of my strengths and superpowers. It became very clear to me that you and I are a reservoir of gems of gifts, talents, special abilities, and superpowers. The catch here is that just as gems and precious stones/metals are mined up from underneath the earth, you need to dig deep into yourself to discover what God has deposited inside of you. When this realization hit me at first, I was very excited to get to work to start mining my strengths reservoir. I ended up completing a number of different exercises designed by different thought leaders, and was enlightened even more.

One of the exercises I had done I had learnt from Rick Warren. This one was so awesome! Let me break it down for you so you can join in on the exercise. Segment your age into bits of decades i.e. ages $0 - 10$, $11 - 20$, 20 -30, 40 -50, e.t.c. (that's just an example btw I'm not an aging 50-year old yet) . And then, for each decade, reflect on the areas you were good at and enjoyed doing (that's what strengths are) e.g. singing, dancing, analyzing/crunching numbers, etc. Next, identify what areas show up the most across those decade slots to detect common patterns. Those patterns give a strong indication of what your strengths and gifts are. For example, after completing that exercise, my top common patterns/areas were leading/mentoring others, reading, planning, helping others, dancing , etc.

Another framework I had followed was called the STAARS Method where I had to identify my Skills, Technologies I was familiar with, Assets I possessed, Achievements, Relationships, Reputations, Strengths. These basically reveal resources and assets we've got working for us.

These exercises tell one thing: you can derive lots of insights from your past, one of them being a clear demonstration of your strengths, gifts and talents in action. Being more aware of your strengths, gifts, and talents boosts your sense of value, confidence and respect.

In short, your gifts and strengths are those things you have an innate ability for; those are the things you do the most with the least amount of effort, while it takes others ages or lots of effort to do. The fact is that you have lots of untapped gifts and strengths. So, it's discovery time!

Asking for sincere, honest feedback

Have you heard the saying, *"you can't see the picture when you're in the frame"*? How about this other variation, *"you can't see the label when you're in the jar"* ? You see, there's only so much you can learn about yourself from yourself simply because you have blindspots. Sometimes, you could, consciously or subconsciously belittle your own superpowers/strengths for the sake of being humble; you may fail to acknowledge and realize that those are the same things that make you unique, different and special. On the other hand, because you don't want to lose the acceptance of others you may get tempted, consciously or subconsciously, to overlook your weaknesses and not call them out so you can address them. That's when getting feedback from others comes in handy.

I had gone through the book *"Exceptional: Build Your Personal Highlight Reel and Unlock Your Potential"*, where I received an idea from. And so, I decided to send out customized emails to different people in my life to learn about what they thought were my unique strengths, gifts, and special abilities, as well as weaknesses. These were individuals who had known me for a while, people who I respect and I know want the best for me; people who aren't afraid to be honest and sincere with me.

The responses were very heartfelt and overwhelming. (I actually almost cried; maybe I did or didn't but big boys don't cry – you know!) Not only did I get feedback on what my strengths were, I also had asked for specific examples when I had demonstrated those qualities/behavior. It's just amazing knowing how sometimes people see you differently from the lens with which you see yourself.

Apart from that, on a number of occasions after I am done delivering talks at speaking gigs, I would have folks from the audience come share how impactful my talk was to them. Also, there've been times when friends would call me up to chime in on a situation they're facing and thankfully I'm able to provide a breakthrough idea. Or when someone shares with me how life changing they found one of my writings. All of these just warm up my heart, remind me of my areas of strength and calling, and make me feel like this is what I'm meant for.

The key takeaway for you is this: people in your life and around you can affirm and confirm your gifts and strengths, and that usually helps to build your confidence in what you've got .

Exploring interests/passions

What are your areas of interest? What activities are you passionate about? What lights you up? These are simple, yet profound questions. I remember that some time ago, if you threw them at me, I would struggle to give sufficient answers. That was simply because I hadn't spent time thinking about and exploring my interests and passions. Meanwhile, your interests - especially your passions - have a lot to say about who you are and what you were put on Earth for (i.e., your purpose).

As someone once put it, your passion refers to the activities you do that light you up, while your purpose is that thing you do that lights other people up. Bishop T.D. Jakes once remarked, *"if you can't figure out your purpose then figure out your passion as your passion will lead you to your purpose."* In short, when you're in close touch with what you're deeply passionate about, you can get a glimpse of your purpose.

For example, Dr. Martin Luther King Jr. was passionate about justice and freedom for Black people in America; that was what he stood and fought for and today, he's celebrated around the world for his courageous acts. Same story with Nelson Mandela in South Africa. How about someone like Mother Teresa? She had a big heart for the destitute. Starting from her base in Calcutta, India, she was able to help cater for the needs of those living in poverty. She extended her mission of love and kindness across the globe through organizations she had founded. These people served a huge purpose because they followed that which they were intensely passionate about.

After learning about the connection between passion and purpose, I began obsessing over discovering and exploring my areas of interest/passion. I had always been very keen about my purpose here on Earth, so that balanced it up.

Talking about interests, I never knew I had some innate liking for plays until I visited a theatre sometime ago on two occasions. I really enjoyed it! I've done some 'local acting' in the past but hopefully some day in the future, I'll join Denzel Washington in the movie industry to make some big hits (who knows where this interest will lead me). Besides that, I am also very passionate about impacting the lives of others in a profoundly positive way, helping them to achieve their goals and to become the best versions of themselves. Gratefully, I get to do that through talks that I deliver at events as well as through my writings.

In the course of this self-discovery journey, these are some of my interest/passion areas I've discovered so far that light me up and light others up. This is an ongoing process and I'm always excited about learning new interests/passions while I seek opportunities to light up the world with those ones I already know about.

The key takeaway for you is that by exploring your interests and passions, not only will you get to know yourself more, you can get an idea about your life's purpose and things you care deeply for.

"The best way to find yourself is to lose yourself in the service of others." — Mahatma Gandhi

Developing, unleashing and maximizing the gifts/strengths

Knowing is one thing. Acting on what we know is another thing. In fact, that's the ultimate thing. After garnering all these insights about gifts, talents, strengths, passions and purpose, there are usually going to be some intersection points which would then become the area of focus. For example, once I got some clarity on all of those, I decided to get to work, developing my gifts and strengths so I can serve others and fulfill purpose; this is what gives life meaning and fulfillment. That's why for the past few years now, I've mostly been focusing on developing my skills in the areas of speaking, writing, and mentorship/leadership, looking for opportunities to serve others.

You may have heard of the law of use and disuse - which simply states that what you use develops and gets stronger with time, but what you don't use shrinks and weakens. This is the main reason you want to spend ample time and resources to develop and unleash your gifts and talents. If you don't develop them, if you don't share them with the world, not only would you not feel great about yourself, you would also be depriving someone out there of that special thing which God put inside of you to deliver to the world. In short, you would be doing the world a disservice if you fail to serve others with your special gifts and strengths.

I've learnt that everyone is created for significance and contribution. It's in using your gifts/talents to serve others that you find fulfillment and meaning in life. Hence, the need to discover, unleash and maximize your gifts, talents and strengths.

"A man's gift makes room for him and brings him before great men." - Proverbs 18:16, NKJV

Identify your core values

If you haven't done so ever, then it's definitely essential that you consider spending some time to figure out what your core values are. To keep things simple, you can pinpoint about 3-5 of them which will guide the decisions you make and reflect the person you really are at your core.

After about three iterations, I finally stuck to these 3 core values: Courage, Self-discipline, and Impact. I believe that sticking to these will help me stay consistent in pursuing my purpose/wildest dreams/ audacious goals across all areas of my life, and push me to become the best version of myself, so I can give my best to the world.

For a list of core values to pick from, you may check out this Core values list (the link is also in the "Resources" section at the end of the book).

Bringing it all together

Those are the key elements of the self-discovery journey I had embarked on. Interestingly, after studying the lives of a number of the thought leaders in the personal development industry, I noticed a lot of similarities in their own self-discovery journey.

Furthermore, not only has the process dramatically raised my level of self-awareness, it has also helped me to understand others better; hence, the improvement in my Emotional Intelligence (I had been emotionally dull before doing this). I hope you get the chance to explore this journey, as well as experience a transformation in your life like I and many others have. Once you've completed the journey, it helps to revisit your dreams/goals to ensure that they're congruent with your findings from the journey exercise.

One thing I believe about identity is that it is not just about who you are, but also a concept/image of who you want to become. This means that we can formulate and build that concept/image. When it comes to defining and building a healthy identity, there are a number of key component structures that are very essential. It's just like constructing a high-rise building. Not only does the foundation have to be solid, pillars have to be put in place to support the building. In the next chapter, I touch on those key pillars for building a healthy, true identity, and how you can strengthen them to build the rock solid identity that you require.

Action exercises

1. If you already haven't done anything close to the self-discovery process outlined in this chapter, mark out a time in your calendar when you'll begin.

2. Segment your age into bits of decades i.e. ages 0 – 10 , 11 – 20, 20 -30, 40 -50, e.t.c. (that's just an example btw I'm not an aging 50-year old yet) . And then, for each decade, reflect on the areas you were good at and enjoyed doing (that's what strengths are) e.g. singing, dancing, analyzing/crunching numbers, etc. Identify what areas show up the most across those decade slots to detect common patterns. Those patterns give a strong indication of what our strengths and gifts are.

3. Using the STAARS Method (acronym for Skills, Technologies familiar with, Assets possessed, Achievements, Relationships, Reputations, Strengths), write down items you've got that fall into those buckets. These basically reveal resources and assets you've got working for you.

4. After completing the exercises in the self-discovery process, what 1-3 gifts/talents/strengths/passions would you focus on exploring?

5. As it's been said that you can't see the picture when you're in the frame; neither can you see the cookies when you're in the cookie jar; that's because everyone has blindspots. That being said, pick 5-10 people in your life to learn about what they think are your unique strengths, gifts, and special abilities, as well as weaknesses. These are individuals who have known you for a while, people who you respect and you know want the best for you; people who aren't afraid to be honest and sincere with you. Also, ask them for specific examples when you have demonstrated those qualities/behaviors.

6. What 1-3 interests/passions of yours are you willing to start exploring to further learn about yourself?

7. How can you begin serving others in the areas of your strengths & gifts? Where will you be doing this and when do you plan to start?

Chapter 3
Reinforce the identity pillars

"You have to be willing to go to war with yourself and create a whole new identity." – David Goggins

When it comes to building an identity that resonates with our core, there are a number of areas that require attention. It's more like the work required in construction. There's usually the work of laying down the foundation, and then setting up the structures that'll support the tower or skyscraper that is being built, so that it remains firm and standing for the longest time possible. Same thing for building that new identity. As mentioned in the previous chapter, I believe that identity isn't only about who you are, but also about who/what you want to become. That's the part you get to be intentional about as you develop that best version of yourself, and it is largely a function of what you believe is possible. Doing this is essential to destroying the beliefs that support your old identity and creating new beliefs that will fuel the new identity.

Next, I discuss areas where I believe you want to raise your consciousness and awareness, so you can build that ideal identity of the person you want to become.

"Anything is possible if a person believes." - Mark 9:23

Self-belief

Beliefs are the foundation of all actions, feelings, and thoughts. You end up taking action or not taking action because of an underlying belief system you have. Just as the operating system is to a computer, so is your belief system to your life. The beliefs you hold onto, consciously or subconsciously, were passed down to you from family, close friends, influential figures, and from very emotional experiences you went through. And so it's not usually your fault that some beliefs got passed down to you. However, the onus is on you to identify and get rid of those limiting beliefs that don't serve you, and to reinforce those that do.

As someone who had been paralyzed by self-doubt for the longest while, I know how crucial this topic of self-belief is. I have struggled with lots of doubts around my abilities, my place in this world, my value/ worth, my faith, etc. All of these held me back in many ways and kept me from taking certain actions that would jolt me to a higher level in life.

For example, whenever I attempted to stretch myself to do something I hadn't done before, the imposter syndrome would kick in. I would begin to doubt myself because I feel like I am not good enough, worthy enough, gifted enough, skilled enough, or deserving of getting that thing. This completely held me back for the longest time, until I began learning more about how to tackle that infamous syndrome, as well as the importance of self-belief. I am very happy and excited about the progress I've made so far in this area, looking back at where I was before deep down in the trenches of self-doubt. The same can happen for you. You can get rid of self-doubt and embrace self-belief.

The beliefs you have about yourself determine the actions you take, which in turn, produces the result you obtain; and the result feeds back into your beliefs.

For example, say you're looking to launch and promote a service you're very passionate about. If you don't believe in yourself that you have what it takes to serve and deliver massive value to your prospective clients, and you further yield to the imposter syndrome telling you that you're not worthy and good enough to meet your clients needs; you're not qualified to serve, and you don't even have the funds to launch; then you'll most likely put in a weak effort towards the promotion. Consequently, with the weak effort, the result will most likely be weak and unimpressive. This poor result then validates the initial belief you had had about yourself.

The converse is also the case. When you believe in yourself that you can make it happen, and you smack down the imposter syndrome, you'll undoubtedly put in a strong effort towards the launch, and definitely, you'll get a positive result. Seeing this result, your self-belief gets a good treat, and you're now ready to put in even more effort to repeat the cycle again and even bigger subsequently.

I remember watching a video clip by Eric Thomas, aka ET, aka The Hiphop preacher, who's considered one of the top motivational speakers in the world (he's one of my faves in the industry). He had shared how at the early stage of his speaking career, he didn't believe in himself, and that negatively affected his performance on stage. Eventually, he learnt the power of self-belief, applied it to his life, and see where he is now. The guy is like a firehose, quenching every flame of doubt or boredom in the mind of his audience.

Just like ET, when I started speaking on stages, I equally didn't believe in myself - and it was very clear even to my audience - as my confidence level was usually low. In fact, on one occasion, someone had seen a promo video I had created for an event I was to speak at. The person remarked that I wasn't confident, just by watching the video - it was very obvious. The moment I began believing in myself, my confidence rose, and I became an entirely different person on stage. I've had people share very positive feedback on my performance ever since. Obviously, I am not perfect, but I know that something changed significantly the moment I began to believe more in myself.

What that means for you is that the more you believe in yourself, the higher your confidence and hence your performance at whatever you do.

How to revamp your self-belief

1. Audit your current beliefs

A good place to start is to write down all the beliefs
you have about yourself that you've been operating
on - positive or negative. Then as you visit each belief,
ask yourself, "does this belief serve me in a positive
way?" If the answer is "yes", then you get to keep and
reinforce it. However, if the answer is "no", then you
want to get rid of it so it doesn't wreck you any further.

2. Get rid of limiting beliefs

One of the main reasons you may doubt yourself is
because you have certain limiting, false beliefs which
you just haven't dug deep enough to confront. The
more of these limiting beliefs that you bust, the higher
your self-belief will rise. I had learnt a method of
busting limiting beliefs from a workshop taught by
Tony Robbins, which I use in clearing limiting beliefs.
I believe it will be very beneficial for you. Here are the
steps:

> i . **Identify an old limiting belief**
> This could be "I am not good enough",
> "Nobody cares for me", "I don't have what it
> takes to land that contract", etc

ii. **Outline the consequences of that belief**

How has holding onto that belief cost you? What beautiful and awesome things have this limiting belief kept you from experiencing in your life? If you continue to hold onto that belief, where do you see yourself in the next couple of years?

iii. **Formulate a new empowering belief**

Given the limiting belief you've been holding onto, what's the opposite that you choose to believe? What belief resonates with you and makes you feel alive? For example, if your limiting belief was "I am not enough", the new empowering belief could be "I am more than enough."

iv. **Get clear on how this new belief will change your life**

This is helpful as it associates emotions with this new belief, and that will help make it to stick. You achieve powerful results when your emotions are involved. Having created this new, empowering belief, how will it change your life and bring in more joy, fun, and excitement to you and to those involved?

v. **Demonstrate why the new belief is true**

Pinpoint at least 3 examples why this new belief is true. These will serve as evidence to prove that your new belief is legit.

vi. **Make it into a habit**

Now that you have your new belief, you want to condition your mind to believe this new truth. A good way to do this is by speaking this new belief over yourself repeatedly until it is ingrained in your subconscious mind. You can consider doing this while walking, jogging, or exercising 30-60mins for the next 66 days. Studies show that it takes about 66 days to form a new habit; hence that figure.

3. Take uncomfortable actions

In addition to the belief busting technique shared earlier, I have also found that taking uncomfortable actions help raise my self-belief. Whenever I feel certain doubts about myself and still resolve to act in spite of that doubt, my self-belief increases and I get excited about taking some more actions to break through that next level of doubt. And this in turn takes my self-belief to a higher level. Taking uncomfortable actions will help to break ceilings/walls of limitation that may have held you back from entering the next level.

4. Believe in something bigger than yourself

One thing that has helped me a lot with raising my self-belief is knowing that I am being guided by a Power that's bigger than me. As a person of faith I believe that God is guiding my steps, and this gives me more reason to believe in myself because I know that He also believes in me. Irrespective of what you believe in, the Universe, Nature, etc, knowing that you're being guided on life's journey can help raise your self-belief and move you to act - even when unsure.

Self-belief affirmations

- *I believe in myself and I expect to excel.*
- *I am confident .*
- *Whatever my mind can conceive and believe I can achieve.*
- *I am unstoppable. I am limitless.*
- *I can. I will. I must. Watch me make it happen.*

- *I am capable of handling everything that comes my way.*

"What we can or cannot do, what we consider possible or impossible, is rarely a function of our true capability. It is more likely a function of our beliefs about who we are." - Tony Robbins

Self-image

What you believe about yourself determines to a huge degree the image you have of yourself. Consequently, the image you have of yourself, determines how you carry yourself and behave in the presence of others. For example, if you see yourself as a "nobody" and you are unduly hard on yourself and don't respect yourself, you'll subconsciously put out that vibe to the people around you. And sadly, once they pick up that vibe, guess what? They'll be tempted to treat you the way you treat yourself, because you just gave them the permission to do that by the way they've seen you carry and treat yourself. The converse is the case. Apart from that, your self-image can affect your performance in the different roles/areas of your life e.g. your job, business, family, relationship, etc.

I know exactly how it feels living with an unhealthy self-image. For a long time, I had seen myself as a "nobody". I had an image of myself as this tiny, little boy who was overlooked, looked down on, ignored, and sometimes, trampled on by others. This continued to some degree in my early young adulthood. As you would imagine, with this unhealthy self-image, the vibe I exuded sometimes to people around me seemed to have given them permission to treat me in an insignificant manner. The fact that I was very timid compounded the matter, because at times I hesitated to stand up for myself when needed, and then people would take advantage of me and throw more sand of disrespect in my face.

Thankfully, as I began working on myself and learning that I was (and still am) a "somebody" (not even because of anything else but mostly for Whose I am), I began designing and living a healthy self-image. Undoubtedly, the aura that I started radiating was different. By doing this alone, not only did I see an improvement across various areas of my life; I also noticed that people started treating me differently, having observed a difference in how I treated myself. And it all started with me upgrading my self-image.

The bottomline is that the image you have of yourself, determines how you carry yourself which in turn determines how people will see and treat you.

How to upgrade your self-image

1. Give yourself the gift of forgiveness and grace

Are you usually very hard on yourself? Maybe you're the typical perfectionist that hardly gives yourself a slack because you take life too seriously as a do-or-die affair. For this reason, you beat yourself up and beat yourself down at the slightest mistake you make; and this is causing you a lot of misery and is further distorting your self-image. Interestingly, you treat other people to the gifts of grace and kindness, but deprive yourself of these beautiful gifts. I know exactly how that feels. Seeing how damaging this was to my self-image especially, I decided some time ago that I was going to quit this forever and never look back. That's been one of the best decisions I've made in my life. I've learnt to be kind, compassionate and gracious to myself, as to that little boy, because, just like everyone else, I deserve those lovely gifts - and so do you! So whenever I make any mistakes - little or grand - I don't beat myself up and down like I used to. Instead, I forgive myself and extract the lessons from that failing experience, as I decide to apply it to the next experience to avoid repeating the same mistake. And then, I move on. You too are worthy and deserving of these amazing gifts of forgiveness, grace and kindness; so begin seeing yourself that way. Don't deprive yourself of those gifts anymore.

2. Respect yourself

What usually happens when you follow through to do what you said you would do? You respect yourself even more, right? And what effect do you think this has on your self-image? Of course, it upgrades your self-image because now you see yourself as someone who is reliable, trustworthy, and has integrity. These are highly valuable qualities which, as people see you radiate, will make them respect you even more; which will add some more points to your level of self-image scores. Consider practicing whatever behaviors you believe would boost your self-respect (e.g. doing what you say you would do, etc.), as those would undoubtedly upgrade your self-image in turn.

3. Find the right possibility/role model

Sometimes it's difficult to imagine what you want to become if you haven't seen a clear image of what's possible. This is where having the right possibility/role model comes into the picture. Looking at the different areas of your life e.g. career, family, business, personal, etc, when you think about the image of the person you want to become, who comes to mind? What qualities and characteristic traits about the person(s) piques your interest the most and why? How can you integrate those traits into your own image while maintaining your own core essence and values? How would you feel and look doing that?

After getting some clarity on what I wanted in the different areas of my life, I decided to design a vision board where I tagged images of some of my "superheroes" or more precisely, my role/possibility models. Each image embodies qualities or skills that I valued and would like to attract more of to my life. For example, I have a picture of my dad who is one of the most humble and amazing people I've ever known; so his picture embodies humility which I value and appreciate. Also, Brian Tracy's picture hangs on my vision board. He is one of the top professional speakers, coaches and writers in the world. I just admire the way he carries himself on the stage as he speaks. Plus, when it comes to the area of writing, speaking and coaching (these are areas I'm working on mastering), I've learnt a truckload from his experiences and teachings. There are obviously other role/ possibility models whose pictures aren't on my vision board but I greatly admire them and they continue to help shape my self-image.

By having the right role/possibility models, you can clearly create a healthy self-image and deeply believe that you can make the representation of the image(s) become a reality. The role models give you this conviction that, "If they can do it, then I can do it too!"

4. Apply the Alter Ego Effect

This was one practice that completely changed my life. I had always struggled with self-doubt and a poor self-image, which obviously made me feel terrible. However, as I began to practice a number of techniques, some of which I already shared earlier, I noticed a gigantic change - especially as I started seeing myself as being the best version of myself. It's a term called the alter ego effect. That is when you mentally shift your identity to match with the adorable qualities or "superpowers" of someone or something else who can empower you to achieve the results you want. I believe that every single one of us has that best/ideal version of ourselves i.e. our alter ego persona. For example, Beyonce's alter ego persona is Sasha Fierce. Kobe Bryant's is Black Mamba. Martin Luther King Jr used the Distinguished Self as his.[1]

The alter ego persona or the ideal YOU is that version of you that excites you and gives you the chills each time you visualize it. That's the version of you that possesses all the valuable rockstar attributes, qualities, skills and characteristics which will enable you to achieve your dreams (they may be similar traits that you admire in your role/possibility model). That's the version of you that's doing the things that you've always dreamed of doing. That's the "ideal YOU" aka your alter ego persona.

Each time you visualize yourself being that person, your self-image soars. In fact, your self-image soars even higher as you intentionally decide to act like that person each day, until the picture of your persona becomes your reality. And that's when you see yourself walking the path of the best version of yourself - the royalty, warrior, hero/heroine and superstar that you're meant to become.

If you don't already have an image of the ideal YOU/ alter ego persona, begin painting it now. How does that person carry himself/herself? How does that person talk and walk? How does that person relate to people? What are the exceptional traits/superpowers the person possesses that blow everyone's mind away ? Just pick something for now and stay open to changing it; it doesn't have to be perfect. Regularly feed your mind with the picture of that best version of yourself. Visualize your ideal YOU and strive to live that out each day.

5. Dress up like a boss

The way we look i.e. clothes we wear, the hairstyle we put on, etc, has an effect on our self-image. For example, did you notice how wearing a suit/jacket for an interview made you feel, compared to the time you wore a T-shirt instead? Research has shown that the clothes we wear affect our mood and self-image. In fact, scientists call this phenomenon - enclothed cognition. That is why it's necessary for the glasses-wearing nerdy, Clark Kent, to remove those glasses, put on his blue and red costume and make his hair, so he can become Superman and go save the day. Exactly the same person but different looks and hence, different effects.

In the same way, ascertain what kind of clothings boost your self-image and make you feel like a superhero or a boss, then put them on - especially when you really need to show up. Not only will this impact the way you see yourself, it will also affect how others perceive you and hence, boost your performance.

Self-image affirmations

- *I forgive myself for past mistakes and failures.*
- *I am beautifully, artistically and wonderfully made by my Creator .*
- *I am a masterpiece and I deserve the best.*
- *I am more than enough.*
- *I am royalty. I am a warrior. I am a superstar.*

"The person we believe ourselves to be will always act in a manner consistent with our self-image." - Brian Tracy

Self-acceptance

Do you feel comfortable under your own skin? Are there parts of your body, your identity or your past that you haven't yet owned up to and embraced wholly? Perhaps that's the reason you keep wishing you had blue eyes or a pointed nose. Or that you were light-skinned or tall like Michael Jordan . Or you keep wishing you were born in a different country or into a different family. You fantasize about all these and each time you wake up to see your reality you get angry with yourself and your Creator for making you this way. This is where self-acceptance comes in. It is our ability to accept ourselves for who we are and for our attributes - whether they are positive or negative. Without this, we will probably live the rest of ourselves very unhappy and miserable.

When I was in my teens, I remember not being happy about various parts of my body; obviously this made me feel very insecure. I wished I had a pointed nose like most Westerners (I watched a lot of Western movies growing up). I also wished I had open teeth (i.e. a space in between my upper incisors) just like one of my neighbors back then, so I would look like a cool kid. In fact, I obsessed over this that I would force toothpicks in between my upper incisors with the hopes of forming an artificial space (hilarious but true! Thankfully I didn't hurt myself). Also, on a number of occasions, I had wished that I was born in a different country. My teenage brain just had a lot of wishes to do a full-blown overhaul on my person.

As I grew older and began to understand how intentional and particular the Creator is about all that He creates, it became clear to me that every single part of my being and identity was made like that for a reason. I believe the same is true for you as well. Nothing about you is an accident.

When you accept all of who you are just as you are - your strengths and weaknesses, your positives and negatives - you no longer yearn for the approval of others. You acknowledge that you are neither perfect nor defective but you can always improve. Also, if you're going to accept yourself as you really are, then you want to know who you really are. You can spend time learning more about your strengths and weaknesses, your desirable and not-so-desirable qualities, etc. Having this awareness is definitely liberating.

How to enhance your self-acceptance

1. Be kind and compassionate to yourself

Although you are products of our past, you mustn't allow your past to imprison or define you. One of the sure ways to not let your past define you is by practicing unconditional self-acceptance. According to Russell Grieger, an internationally-recognized leader in the theory and practice of Rational Emotive Behavior Therapy, (REBT), *"unconditional self-acceptance is understanding that you are separate from your actions and your qualities. You accept that you have made mistakes and that you have flaws, but you do not let them define you"*. [2]

When you realize that you are not the bad actions that you took or the failures that you experienced, it becomes easier for you to let go of every guilt and shame so you can move on. Holding onto guilt and shame does no one any good. Obviously, the main caveat here is that you learn from your mistakes as you continue to improve on your not-so-desirable qualities/ traits/skills, so you can make better decisions moving forward.

You and I are not perfect and as a matter of fact, no one else is perfect. You're doing the best that you can with what you have at the moment. So, be kind and compassionate to yourself.

2. Embrace what makes you unique

You have strengths and weaknesses and that's part of what makes you who you are. As a way of reinforcing how unique and special you are, I believe that it's important that you identify and celebrate your strengths/superpowers and not wait for others to do it. In the same vein, it's equally essential that you acknowledge your weaknesses because that's the first step to self-improvement. The more you own up to your weaknesses while working on improving or delegating them, the less insecure I believe you'll feel. That's because you mostly already know what your critics, internal or external, may want to tease you about.

3. Be grateful for what you've got

After learning about the stories of various individuals with disabilities who, in spite of disability, accepted themselves and went around impacting the lives of others, it became clear to me that I have no excuse to not accept myself.

I am reminded of the story of Nick Vujicic who was

born without limbs; he literally has no arms and legs. But guess what? Not only is he excited about life; he travels around the world inspiring and encouraging others to live a great life with purpose and passion. He is the founder of the Life Without Limbs as well as Attitude is Altitude movements, and has written a number of books. From some of his fun videos I've seen online, he's truly living his best life. Although, at the early stage of his life, he couldn't accept the way he looked, he was inspired by the story of a man with disability. Nick chose to be grateful for the life he had and the way he was, as there were others in the worst of conditions who were still doing great things with their lives.

Recently, I also got to know about another Nick with a similar story; his full name is Nick Santonastasso. He was born with only one arm and no legs; his one arm though only has one finger. Guess what? Nick didn't let any of that define him or hold him back from pursuing his dreams. He has ventured into different areas including writing, wrestling, bodybuilding, fashion, etc. He now travels around the world inspiring and empowering people to overcome the victim mentality and live the kind of life they love. How amazing!

Whenever you feel unhappy about a part of your body or a deficiency you think you have, I hope you're inspired by the stories of the Nicks along with those of the incredible individuals with disabilities who are inspiring lives around the world. What can you be grateful for?

4. Look for the good in what you can't change

You see, for every fixed part of our body or identity that we are uncomfortable with, especially those that can't be changed ever or easily, there are two options, at least from my purview. One, it's either you look for the good in it and accept it. Or, two, you live with it in vexation and complaint for the rest of your life. I don't know about you, but the latter seems miserable, although I understand that the former can be very hard to take in.

When she was nineteen months old, Helen Keller lost her senses of sight and hearing due to an illness. While this was enough reason for her to give up on life, complain and go ballistic about why this ordeal hit her, Helen made up her mind to go against all odds and make something good out of her situation. With the help of her mentor and teacher, Anne Sullivan, Helen Keller learnt to read, write, speak and listen to others - which was an incredible feat for someone labeled deaf. Even with her disability, she accomplished some great feats during her lifetime including: writing 14 books; becoming the first deaf-blind person to earn a bachelor's degree; acting as an activist for people with disabilities; getting inducted into 2 Hall of Fame recognitions. Not only did she accept herself even with her condition, she became a voice and an inspiration to everyone, especially those with disabilities. Her life eloquently communicates the fact that your disability - whether it is physical or otherwise - isn't a liability or a hindrance. It can become one of your greatest assets if you own it while making the most of your life.

Something good can come out from the "not-so-good" parts of our lives.

Self-acceptance affirmations

- *I accept myself as I am including my flaws, my imperfections, my strengths and my weaknesses.*
- *I am not the actions that I take - good or bad*
- *I am not defined by my past, my weaknesses, or other people's approval or opinions of me.*

- *I am not my successes neither am I my failures.*

"Accept everything about yourself; I mean everything. You are you and that is the beginning and the end, no apologies, no regrets."
– Henry A. Kissinger

Self-love

This one may seem a bit cheesy at first, but take it from someone who had struggled with self-love that indeed, it is very essential to building a healthy identity. To kick things off, self-love goes beyond doing lovely, sweet things to make ourselves look good on the outside or to spoil ourselves with a good treat. I believe it's more of an inside game. Actually, according to psychologists, self-love has four sub components, and violating any one of them could negatively impact overall self-love [3]. The four sub components are :

1. **Self-awareness**: a key element of emotional intelligence. It's being conscious of how your thoughts trigger certain emotions/feelings which move you to taking action in a particular way. Negative thoughts

trigger negative emotions, which invariably leads to negative actions. The contrast is the case with positive thoughts. Positive actions usually result from positive emotions/feelings which were birthed by positive thoughts.

2. **Self-worth:** a perception of how valuable and worthy you believe you are. You've been blessed with endless potentials but sometimes, you may struggle to see what those are. That's why when you think that you're not valuable or worthy, you may feel unloved and so you struggle with loving yourself in turn. But certainly, you are beyond worthy and valuable because indeed, you have something special, unique and valuable to offer the world.

3. **Self-esteem:** a measure of the confidence/respect you have for yourself, usually based on your achievements or some super qualities you possess. It is very closely knitted with self-worth in the sense that your level of self-esteem rises whenever your self-worth goes up. There is usually a tendency to love and appreciate yourself more when you feel an elevated sense of self-esteem.

4. **Self-care:** this is undoubtedly the part that comes to mind when you hear self-love. It's mostly the way you "spoil" yourself just as you would do for someone

you've fallen head over heels for. (I am sure you know exactly what I am talking about here so no further explanation for this one.)

Understanding and effectively managing these sub components can clearly affect your self-love. The more love you can give to yourself, the more love others can receive from you. After all, that's what, I believe, life is all about - giving and receiving love.

How to reignite the passion of your self-love

1. Forgive yourself and forgive others

I believe this is the starting point to getting self-love. It can be hard and even impossible to love the person you see in the mirror when you're holding some form of guilt or bitterness against that person. Irrespective of what happened in the past, whether or not it was your fault, I am hoping you can forgive yourself. It can be difficult, but it is worth it. Studies have shown that forgiveness wards off anger, depression, stress and anxiety; it also promotes optimism. In the end, it's for your own good. After you've forgiven yourself, you give yourself the permission to forgive others who may have wronged you. There's lots of peace, freedom and liberation that comes from forgiveness.

2. Accept yourself

One thing I'm persuaded about is that to truly love yourself, it is necessary that you accept yourself for who you are. It is with this acceptance (think unconditional self-acceptance mentioned earlier) that you literally give yourself the permission to love "You" for who you truly are. Accepting yourself is a way of saying that you're worthy of love and so, you won't withhold it from yourself. And, of course, this acceptance comes from knowing yourself.

3. Show love to others

I've learnt that self-love isn't you being selfish, looking out only for yourself. It can greatly be promoted when you show love to others around you. When you observe that you're showing love to others, you tell yourself that you're loving and caring and that way, you can easily give that same love to yourself. When you give what you want the most, it will come back to you in large measures. Mind you, this doesn't completely annul the saying that you can't give what you don't have. I believe that everyone has a seed of love, and a heart to love but sometimes we withhold love from ourselves but not from others. However, in the course of loving others, you can come to realize that you too are deserving of love.

4. **Take good care of yourself**

This one goes beyond just giving yourself a treat to a spa or classy restaurant or expensive vacay (all of which are super great, btw). I believe it also includes having the right nutrition, sufficient sleep, exercising, etc. Same way you would care for someone/something you love dearly should be the same way you treat yourself. This also entails setting proper boundaries - personal, work - as well as saying 'no' to certain things so you can say 'yes' to giving yourself the care you deserve, so that you are able to care for those around you.

Self-love affirmations

- *I like myself .*
- *I am loved dearly by my Creator and I matter.*
- *I am worthy and deserving of receiving great love.*
- *I forgive myself; I forgive others and I move on.*
- *My successes don't make me love myself more and my failures don't make me love myself any less* (this will

sound better when used in the third-party).

"How you love yourself is how you teach others to love you." —
Rupi Kaur

Self-talk

Self-talk is, more or less, the story you tell yourself about who you are and what you are capable of doing and becoming. The main reason this is very essential in building a healthy identity is that your words, being powerful beyond your imagination, create your reality.

What you say about yourself ends up becoming a self-fulfilling prophecy. Inasmuch as other people can speak positive and powerful things to/over you, what you speak to/over yourself trumps everything else anyone says - whether positive or negative.

Furthermore, self-talk has a significant effect on your performance in the different areas of your life. In fact, studies have shown this to be true even in the world of sport.

I love what, author and former law professor at the

University of California, Toni Bernhard, wrote about self-talk:

"Harmful self-talk can take many forms, some of which come under the heading of what are called cognitive distortions. Cognitive distortions are errors in thinking that lead you to talk to yourself in irrational ways. This can take many forms. Here are a few: exaggerating things way out of proportion; taking everything personally; holding yourself to unrealistically high standards; assuming that you know why others act or speak as they do." [4]

Honestly, I have fallen prey to all 4 of those forms of cognitive distortions she shared. That negatively impacted my inner self-talk and hence the quality of my life. Thankfully, by practicing positive, healthy self-talk, I was able to break that negative pattern; hence, the quality of my life has improved drastically and continues to.

How to improve your self-talk

1. Silence the inner critic

It is worth being intentional about identifying the

words you speak to yourself, especially the voice of the inner critic. Sometimes you may get critical about yourself when the voice of the inner critic gets very loud, mostly because you're completely engrossed in your own head, thinking that the world revolves around you . You can nudge yourself out from this illusion by taking the spotlight away from yourself and focusing it on others. That's a term known as self-transcendence which, according to research, can help reduce self-criticism. [5]

I've seen this happen over and over again, especially when I'm getting ready to climb a stage to give a talk, creating a pep-talk video to post on social media, or even writing a book (like I am doing right now). Whenever the spotlight is on myself, I can loudly hear the inner critic say statements like - "Can you still remember what the last point is for that speech you're delivering? Don't go up there and disgrace yourself." Or "Do you really know what you're talking about in the video you're creating? No one pays attention to crappy videos." Or "Why would anyone want to read this book you're writing?" I definitely don't want to yield to any of these, so, instead of trying to argue back-and-forth, I just switch the spotlight to focus on the people I am called to serve, thinking about how best I can provide value and impact. And in most cases that voice dwindles. Of course, I address the critics in my work while putting in effort to serve readers/ listeners of my work with the intention of positively impacting their lives.

So the next time you hear the voice of the inner critic, consider switching your focus away from yourself and toward those you're called to serve.

2. **Be mindful of what you focus on**

The thoughts you focus on determine how you feel; and what you feel, you speak out. You may not always be able to control the wave of thoughts that hit you throughout the day, nor can you control how people behave towards you, but you can control how you respond to those. For this reason, it always helps, as much as possible, to interpret both your behaviors and that of others through a positive lens, as that will to a very large extent affect your self-talk.

For example, if you make a mistake while working on a task, instead of saying - "I am so stupid, I never do things right" - how about saying something like, "This is not great, but I know I am not perfect. I will learn from this error and ensure not to repeat it again." One focuses on beating yourself down - which honestly isn't helpful - while the other focuses on acknowledging the mistake and making improvements.

Another example is when responding to someone else's behavior. Let's say some driver cuts you off while driving, or honks crazily at you for no justifiable reason (I'm sure you know how that feels). Instead of saying to yourself, "That driver is an amateur and needs to be whipped; in fact, his/her license needs to be seized" ; how would it sound saying, "That driver must be having a bad day; maybe he/she is rushing to attend to an emergency."

In both cases, you may also notice that the story you tell yourself based on what you had focused on about those behaviors/incidents drives your reaction at the end of the day. Giving yourself and others the benefit of the doubt while interpreting events in a positive light has a role it plays in your self-talk.

3. **Re-program your self-talk**

In this quest to improve self-talk, there's no better ally to enlist than the mind - by leveraging the power of affirmations (more on affirmations in the next chapter). First thing here is to identify the undermining, negative self-talk statements that have been prevalent in your life. Then decide that you want to replace them by empowering, positive self-talk statements. Once you've identified the new self-talk statements, you want to write them down somewhere you can view them regularly. Also, you want to repeat them over and over again to engrain them in your subconscious so they come naturally to you.

There are two options to consider to make this happen. One, do the mirror exercise. This is where you stand in front of the mirror and literally speak those new empowering, positive self-talks statements to yourself. Two, recite those positive self-talk statements into a voice recorder and then play the recording to yourself regularly. The more you speak your new self-talk statements over yourself with emotions and power, the higher the overall effect it produces. I can't tell you how much of a difference both techniques have had in boosting my mood and hence, my performance. I believe the same can happen for you.

Self-talk affirmations

- *I acknowledge that my words are powerful; so I speak only of those things that I want to attract to my life.*
- *I am kind and compassionate to myself and to others.*

- *I only focus on the positive things that I want to attract in life.*
- *I expect good things to happen to me and through me today.*
- *All things are working for me, not against me.*
- *Today, I choose to be happy.*

"Be very careful what you say to yourself because someone very important is listening ... YOU!" - John Assaraf

You become like those you are surrounded by most of the time. So, a great way by which you can strengthen all 5 areas is to surround yourself with people who are healthy in these areas, or are, at least, intentionally working towards that.

Additionally, you've probably heard it said that you can't give what you don't have. Personally, I can attest to that on multiple levels. On the journey to fulfilling your purpose, you'll constantly be interacting with different kinds of people. If you are going to believe in them, create a healthy image of them, accept them unconditionally, love them, and speak positively to/of them, then you want to first do all those to yourself. That's why these 5 pillars of identity are of paramount importance.

Rome wasn't built in a day. So, you won't be able to build or strengthen all 5 pillars overnight, but you can intentionally work on improving them daily.

Do you know that your words are powerful? In fact, the words you speak regularly often become your reality; I am sure you may have examples of that - positive or negative (I definitely do!).

In the next chapter, I cover a technique that can be leveraged to alter your mood/state and mind, using the power of words. I can't wait to share this with you.

Action exercises

1. What actions can you begin taking from today to improve in the 5 pillars:

> I. Self-belief
> II. Self-image
> III. Self-acceptance
> IV. Self-love
> V. Self-talk

2. Who can you ask to support you in staying consistent with the changes you'll make in those areas?

Chapter 4

Speak it until you see it

"I figured that if I said it enough, I would convince the world that I really was the greatest." - Muhammad Ali

Has there ever been a time in your life when, consciously or subconscious, you repeatedly made remarks about yourself or certain situations in your life, and that which you said became a reality? I definitely can recall instances in my life where that was the case. There have been times when, in my ignorance, I had declared something negative and sadly it happened. And thankfully I've had times when positive things occurred because my declarations were positive as well. This just points to one thing: our words become our reality.

I believe that one of the greatest powers we humans have been given is that of spoken words. The words you speak can either build or destroy your identity and your life. Not only that, your words can also help boost your moods, increase your self-esteem/self-confidence, help you heal, break cycles of negative thinking patterns, and so much more. And so, the onus is on you to only speak forth the things that you'd like to see manifest in your life, not the opposite of that. This is how you get to experience the power of positive affirmation working in your favor.

Why affirmations are powerful and effective

You know that this whole craze about positive affirmation isn't just woo woo, right? There's actually science behind it. The reason positive affirmations work is explained chiefly by the Self-affirmation Theory which proposes that *"people have a fundamental motivation to maintain self-integrity, perception of themselves as good, virtuous, and able to predict and control important outcomes. In virtually all cultures and historical periods, there are socially shared conceptions of what it means to be a person of self-integrity, which means that one perceives oneself as living up to a culturally specified conception of goodness, virtue, and agency."* [1]

This theory hinges on the fact that the words you affirm are tied to these two key concepts: one, self-integrity which is simply your perceived ability to keep to your words and act in ways that will reward you with feeling worthy, and deserving of praise and acknowledgement; two, self-identity (notice the word 'identity' showing up here) is the story you tell yourself about who you are - good, competent, flexible, adaptive, etc. And so, consciously and/or unconsciously, in an attempt to maintain your self-integrity and self-identity, you are more inclined to match your actions to your words.

In addition, there is also research showing that practicing affirmations actually creates neural pathways in the part of the brain that stores information about personal valuation and sense of self [2]. And so, the more you repeat those affirmations (e.g. "I am confident", "I am a person of value", etc), the more you program and ingrain them in your brain until they become your reality.

That said, affirmations along with the law of attraction and spiritual principles explain why your words, being powerful, can dictate your reality. So, how powerful are your words again?

"Affirmations are our mental vitamins, providing the supplementary positive thoughts we need to balance the barrage of negative events and thoughts we experience daily." — *Tia Walker*

How to compose your own affirmations

So, I am a very big fan of Tony Robbins. His work has had a profound impact in my life. I've learnt a lot from the big guy. While attending a number of his webinars, I recall him sharing how he had struggled growing up: his family was poor, he didn't feel loved, he got massively overweight at one point and lost self-esteem, amongst many other forms of hardships he had faced. Tony developed his own affirmation routine (he prefers the word incantations instead to emphasize the importance of engaging the whole body and emotions while affirming the words) which he kept on repeating to himself for years until they became his reality. For example, while he was young and broke, he started affirming words like - "I am one with God. God's wealth and abundance are flowing through me..." - until that poor, broke teenager became wealthy. Although he is definitely very wealthy now, he probably still says those words to elevate his wealth to another level. He also had affirmations to target other unpleasant situations in his life where he needed a change. And obviously coupled with massive actions and grace, those affirmations become a reality as well. There are stories of many well-known individuals who continue to leverage affirmations to transform their lives.

That said, the starting point of any affirmation is with our current unpleasant situations. Maybe it's a habit, mindset or outcome you're looking to create, reinforce or remove from your life; you would simply build a series of affirmations (or incantations, using Tony Robbins's terms) to address those.

One thing worth noting is that for affirmations to be effective, they would comply with the 3 P's; they would be **positive**, **personal**, and be stated in the **present** tense. For example, as someone who had struggled with self-doubt, I had composed affirmations for that. One of them says, *"I am confident. I am decisive and I believe in myself."* Also, in an attempt to combat an unhealthy comparison habit, I had to come up with this one, *"Today I choose not to compare myself to others. Rather I will focus on my God-given gifts, talents and abilities."* Even though I'm already seeing drastic transformation in those areas, I continue to repeat those affirmations to myself daily along with a host of others until they not only become true, but also become a part of who I am at the core, at the identity level. (Some of my favorite times in the day are times when I do my affirmations.)

Obviously, for each affirmation statement, you definitely want to take consistent actions that are congruent with those words, otherwise your life would be out of harmony. This can lead to unhappiness and sometimes misery. Your life will be in so much harmony and unity when you walk your talk. For a collection of affirmations to use, be sure to check out **rebrand.ly/FreeGiftIdentity** ; it contains a couple of powerful affirmations that I use as well.

Talking about unhappiness and misery, those are also feelings that you can experience when you are frustrated about your identity, feeling like you don't know who you are, lack a sense of purpose, belonging and contribution, and you don't seem to appreciate what you already have. If any of these resonate with you or someone you know then come along with me to the next chapter where I go even deeper on that.

Action exercises

1. What unpleasant habits, mindset, situations or outcomes in your life are you committed to changing?
2. For each item listed above, come up with 1-2 affirmations.
3. What corresponding actions can you begin taking consistently (daily or weekly) to support the affirmations you've just created?

Chapter 5

Stuck in an Identity Crisis?

"Identities were like teeth: hard to maintain and easy to lose, but people tended to look at you funny when you were missing one."
— *Nenia Campbell*

Financial crisis, technological crisis, natural crisis, etc, are examples of crises that occur in the outside world. You would agree with me that these crises can be very ugly and horrific, causing lots of havoc, pain and unhappiness. In the same vein, crises exist in the inner world i.e. within us as humans, and a very common one is the identity crisis. It's when you lack a sense of self, feeling that you don't even know who you are. Undoubtedly, just like the crises in the outside world, the identity crisis can result in unhappiness, frustration, anxiety and in the worst case loss of life, especially when not handled properly. Hence, the gravity of this topic.

Am I going through an identity crisis? (Signs and symptoms)

Unlike medical conditions for which you can pinpoint tangible symptoms like fever, headache, red eyes, etc; it can be quite difficult to spot when someone is being hit with an identity crisis. The person won't suddenly develop swollen cheeks, red eyes, sore skin or tongue, joint pains, etc. Nonetheless, if you relate to multiple items on the following list, then you may actually be in the midst of an identity crisis:

1. Asking questions constantly about who you are, your character, your beliefs, your values
2. Feeling like you don't know yourself
3. Dodging/dreading answering questions about who you are
4. Questioning your purpose, role in society or the world at large and the meaning of life
5. Doubting yourself and your abilities most of the time
6. Getting bored/unfulfilled very easily even after

trying new things at different times

7. Changing your opinion/value radically, most of the time, to match that of others around you especially within relationships or workplace environment, etc (being a chameleon).

8. Experiencing regular episodes of anxiety

I wish I could hand you a master list that'll just diagnose whether or not someone is in the midst of an identity crisis, but I don't know if that'll be exactly perfect. However, from psychological studies and people's stories I know of, along with my own past struggle with identity crisis, those items on the list are on point.

Looking back at the time when I was in the eye of the identity crisis, I literally experienced all the symptoms of the identity crisis outlined above. Virtually everything about my identity was in question - my values, beliefs, character, self-image, self-esteem, purpose/ meaning of life, abilities, concept of relationships, etc. Just so the list doesn't fill up the entire page and bore you to sleep, let's just say that I questioned everything. And because I felt like I had no clue about who I was, I attempted to become someone/something I wasn't - as dictated by external sources.

As you would imagine, that left me feeling super anxious, bored, unhappy, sometimes depressed, but thankfully, I never had suicidal thoughts. Interestingly, I knew about this concept of identity crisis but somehow I was oblivious to the fact that I was in it because a part of me felt that was normal since some of the symptoms had lasted for quite some time. It reached its peak at some period, and I just couldn't take it anymore, so I decided to turn things around. I am grateful to God for a great turnaround which, of course, didn't happen overnight; plus, it wasn't always pleasant but it was indeed necessary.

Causes of identity crisis

According to Erik Erikson's psychosocial theory of human development, identity crisis usually occurs at the stage of identity versus role confusion[1]. This usually happens during periods of sudden transition from an old to new stage in life when an individual is trying to figure out who they are in the new stage and how they can fit in well there. It's failure to get this transition right that usually leads to the crisis.

Although Erikson postulated that this stage occurred in adolescence, in today's fast-changing world we know that identity crisis can happen more often at various points in a person's life. Nonetheless, his explanations for the occurrence, I believe, still hold lots of water.

Some of the life changing/transitional events that could cause the identity crisis include:

1. Lost/change in job or career path
2. Entering/ending a relationship, marriage or partnership
3. Moving to a different city or country
4. Giving birth
5. Losing a family member or close friend
6. Facing a traumatic experience
7. Getting to know about a health condition (affecting oneself or a family member or close friend)

In essence, whenever the source of your identity, i.e. the "label" (it could be a job title, family or societal role, etc) you've clung to and have allowed to define who you are gets shaken or knocked off, there's a potential threat of facing an identity crisis. In my case, one of the major causes of the crisis, at least from what I am currently aware of, was transitioning into the place of my perceived purpose and calling which was different from my area of vocation. And because I struggled a lot with who I currently was and who I would become in that new place, I tried to become someone I wasn't - which didn't pan out well at all.

Essentially, I had witnessed the role confusion which Erikson talked about as to how I fit into society and my contribution to the world, most especially after the transition. Honestly, I have experienced a few other transitional events from that list but, I believe this was a major one for me. That was part of what led me to realize that I was down that deep, dark rabbit hole. So, what can you do to get out of the hole, if you're in there now?

"Throwing your heart into something is great, but when any one thing becomes all that you stand for, you're vulnerable to an identity crisis when you pivot to a Plan B." - Reid Hoffman

Escaping the identity crisis

Based on my personal experiences coupled with research I had done, I have garnered some effective ways to navigate the identity crisis. Obviously, these aren't overnight fixes and, honestly speaking, I believe they're worth continuing even after you feel you're out of the crisis.

1. **Fall in love with gratitude**

In my identity crisis moment, I focused a lot on 3 things: loss, less, never i.e. things I had lost, things I had less of and things I thought I would never get. And this caused me a lot of misery and anxiety that there were several nights that I could barely sleep soundly. All of these got me stressed out and frustrated, causing me to feel sad, mad and bad . To cap it off, I also had a bunch of unmet expectations especially for myself.

Eventually, I had to wake up to the reality that something was wrong, and that a change was needed. So, I set out to find a way out. In all of my findings, virtually everything I stumbled on (podcasts, books, Scriptures, etc) pointed to the same thing that was lacking in my life at the time - Gratitude! Gratitude!! Gratitude!!! Don't get me wrong, I knew what gratitude was - especially as a person of faith who believes in thanking God at all times. One thing I felt was that, especially in that period of my life, I seemed to have only practiced gratitude from my head and not from my heart (Like they say, *"if you're not doing it, then you don't know it well enough."*). I made a decision to deeply learn and practice gratitude with all my whole heart since I was just tired of all the misery.

Although there were many sources that helped me make the shift, this one quote by Tony Robbins struck a chord in me - *"Trade your expectations for appreciation and your whole world changes instantly."* That was a game changer for me. And so, I began focusing on appreciating everything I have and I am so that I have no time to pore over things I don't have. Each morning right after I wake up and while still in bed, I identify 5 things currently in my life that I am grateful for and 5 things that are yet to come into my life. I experience the feeling of having received them already, and give thanks like they're here already (that's giving thanks in advance). I also think about who loves me and who I love. This has become part of my daily routine and, God willing, will remain a lifestyle forever.

What this means for you is that letting go of all those expectations that remind you of what you don't yet have, and then appreciating all that you have is a great way to stay happy, sane and joyful. That's how powerful gratitude is, and I know that for sure.

2. **Quit the comparison game**

Most times you may lose sight of your life's journey because you are so focused on other people's journey that it distracts you from yours. You may belittle where you are and overly magnify where others are, and because you don't have what they have, the comparison villain kicks off negative emotions that leaves you even more depressed and sometimes envious. At least that was the case for me and some other individuals whose identity crisis story I am aware of. Meanwhile, there's no reason for the comparison or competition.

First off, the moment you convince yourself that everyone's journey isn't the same and in fact shouldn't be, I believe that's when things will begin to turn around for good in this area.

Secondly, what makes each person special and unique is different; comparing my unique set of strengths to yours is analogous to comparing apples to oranges - it's a losing comparison every single time because those two most likely won't be the same - and that's fine, because they were never meant to be the same. That's why I believe it helps to embrace what makes you special and unique, as that's what allows your light to become visible and noticeable as it is different from the billion other lights already shining to the world.

Thirdly, you are not in competition with anyone else but yourself. The only person you should strive to be better than tomorrow is the person you are today. And with the first two points being true, we can deduce that every single person has his/her designated, unique place and path to occupy and shine. You have yours and I have mine, so why would anyone want to compete or compare with someone else?

The truth of the matter is that irrespective of where you stand, there will always be people ahead of you. If you only focus on that, then you'll most likely feel inferior, belittled and too discouraged to advance. On the other hand, there will always be people who are behind you. If you fixate on that, you'll get conceited and complacent, and may never stretch to reach your maximum potential. That's why I believe you want to focus on one person - the person you see in the mirror.

I opted out from the comparison game the moment I woke up to all those 3 realizations and I will tell you that I felt so much relief and freedom like never before. I choose to be very happy for everyone where they are, and also for where I am, because I know that our journeys are different. Obviously, I still get tempted to compare myself with others but I remind myself of those 3 convictions each time and strive not to yield to the comparison bidding.

The bottomline is that quitting the comparison game is definitely necessary to end the misery of the crisis.

3. **Take a social media fast**

Although social media has its own benefits (connecting people together, raising awareness of happening events around the world, sharing ideas and content with the world, etc), the one negative thing it has promoted is the comparison game. That's why I believe social media is the last place anyone dealing with an identity issue wants to frequent.

One thing I believe will be very helpful in ending the comparison game is getting off social media at least until those 3 convictions stated in the previous point have been imbibed at heart. When you can see someone advancing successfully in an area of life that you may be struggling in and deep down in your heart you can say that you're genuinely happy for the person and truly mean it, that may just be a sign that the comparison villain is losing its grip on you.

4. Get out of your own world and serve others
In the midst of the identity crisis, along with the anxiety, there was some level of fear that gripped me. It was the fear that I won't get the things I wanted and that I would lose what I had. I was living afraid so I stayed confined in my head and in my little world most of the time. This led me to only think mostly about myself: how I would defend myself from whoever/ whatever was coming to take what I had, and also to pounce on whoever/ whatever wouldn't give me what I wanted. That was where the scarcity mindset emerged from. To me, that is a recipe for unhappiness, misery and lack of fulfillment.

After going through some mindset shifts, I saw how this wasn't serving me and so, I decided to make a change in my life. I once heard someone say that when we give what we want, it would come back to us in truckloads. I yearned for abundance in my life and so I had to make up my mind to give from the little I was manifesting at the time so that I would hopefully receive abundance in large buckets into my life. That spurred me on the journey to get out of my little world to serve others and share more of my resources, especially time, knowledge, gifts, money, etc. This was how I broke free from the scarcity mindset as well (thank God!).

I may not have everything I need right now, but serving others with my resources makes me feel joyful and abundant. I desire more abundance and continue to affirm that each day so that I can keep giving more of that to the world.

So, the next time you feel forgotten, unloved or disheartened, step out of your world and go do something caring, loving and encouraging for others; then watch what happens (Hint: the outcome will be refreshing and rewarding).

5. **Get help**

Les Brown once advised, *"Ask for help not because you're weak but because you want to remain strong. Ask for help and don't stop until you get it"*. That is sage advice, trust me. When I realized what was going on with me at the time, I opened up to a mentor and some very close friends who supported me through the journey. I also joined a number of communities (e.g. small groups at church and virtual personal development groups) for encouragement and motivation. Getting to work with coaches and therapists was also very valuable as I got to uncover a number of unhealthy/limiting beliefs. I also made sure to spend more time doing spiritual practices e.g. praying, meditating on Scriptures, etc to get divine help.

Keeping to yourself in silence - especially in a crisis like this - doesn't help at all. On the other hand, reaching out to people who care, and can help, makes a whole lot of difference and brings a positive change. Asking for help isn't a sign of weakness but in truth it's a sign of real strength. So, if you need help, please go get it right away.

6. **Learn more about yourself**

According to studies, those who get to learn more about themselves i.e. get on the self-discovery journey, etc, end up happier than ever. This is even more applicable for someone dealing with an identity crisis. Chapters 2 - 3 provide guidance on the self-discovery journey which I strongly encourage you to embark on.

You may not always be able to control those transitional events that could trigger an identity crisis, but you can always control how you interpret and handle them when/if they hit you. No matter how unpleasant it may be, I believe that there's a silver lining in this crisis which when navigated properly, can make the next phase of your life the best part of your life.

Action exercises

1. Looking through the list of signs and symptoms of the identity crisis, do you exhibit any of them? (If no, do you know anyone who is?)
2. If you answered "yes" to #1 (for you or that person you had in mind), which of the ideas shared in the section "Escaping the identity crisis" can you begin practicing today ?

Conclusion

"Everybody is a genius. But if you judge a fish by its ability to climb a tree, it will live its whole life believing that it is stupid."
~ Albert Einstein

Big Kudos to you for making it to the end of the book! (You're truly amazing!) I believe that by now you've gotten a better understanding of identity and how you can build yours to the level you require. Hopefully, by going through the exercises, you've learnt a lot more about yourself, your strengths, gifts, and how you can begin using those to serve others. That said, you may be wondering to yourself, now what? What's the point of it all? I am glad you asked.

"The value of identity of course is that so often with it comes purpose." - Richard Grant

Finding fulfillment

According to one of the top peak performance coaches and strategists in the world (if not the top, in my opinion), Tony Robbins, there are two skills everyone needs to master. One, the science of achievement. Two, the art of fulfillment. The science of achievement essentially hinges on the fact that any result we want to achieve takes a process which can be learnt from someone else who has achieved the same result. In other words, since success leaves clues, instead of trying to reinvent the wheel, we can simply model after someone who has done what we want and we'll get similar results. This will save time and effort and avoid unnecessary trial-and-error. The art of fulfillment isn't quite the same. You see, what fulfills you will most likely be different from what fulfills me; this would differ for every single one of us. And that's plainly because purpose and identity differ for each person. Hence the essence of the entire journey we've traveled through the pages of this book.

At the end of the day everyone is in pursuit of this one thing - happiness! True happiness comes from fulfillment. Fulfillment, I believe, comes from pursuing your calling/purpose and giving yourself to serving others with your resources (gifts, talents, special abilities, etc). That's what gives meaning to life and reason to living. But then it can be difficult for you to wholeheartedly give yourself in such service to others when you don't even know who you are.

I strongly believe that we all need to pursue what makes us feel happy, excited and fulfilled and not try to be people-pleasers. It is miserable doing things that don't bring you fulfillment - just to please others and save face. How long would that have to last for? There are myriads of stories of highly successful individuals -at least in the world's eyes - who still didn't feel fulfilled in what they were doing. This is mostly because they didn't connect with the core of who they are and their true purpose. Sadly, a number of them couldn't take it anymore and so, they took their own lives. Tony Robbins captured this perfectly well when he said, *"Success without fulfillment is the ultimate failure."* If you haven't found what makes you fulfilled and excited in life, I encourage you to keep searching for it; I am confident you'll find it. This is definitely a quest worth embarking on. And it all begins with knowing who you are.

"The two most important days in your life are the day you are born and the day you find out why." - Mark Twain

Who are you?

I know I had asked this question in the Introduction chapter but permit me to ask you again - who are you? What will you now allow to define you? I hope that your response connects deeply with the core of who you are, and it's not something that will be stripped off from you by external circumstances. Once you're convinced about who you truly are, your true identity, it behooves you to live it out every single day to the best of your abilities. When you know who you are with certainty, you'll automatically know who you're not. You can then stop answering to those lies and start living out your truths unapologetically.

One last message

Be yourself

I am sure I had hinted at this multiple times in this book, I still feel the need to capture it again here - be yourself. Get comfortable living under your own skin and stop wishing you were someone else. I believe that everyone has a unique place and purpose to fill in the world. Why try to squeeze yourself inside someone else's occupied space when yours has been reserved and it's waiting for you?

You're at your best being yourself than trying to be someone else because 'You' fits you best.

Remember that you're beautifully, artistically, uniquely, specially created for a purpose. Just as you are, you matter. You're more than enough; you're worthy, and you have something special and unique to give to the world. So, choose yourself. Know yourself. Accept yourself. Love yourself. Value yourself. Appreciate yourself. Be yourself.

It was really a pleasure taking this journey with you. Be sure to check out the sections for "Resources" and "Recommended readings". I believe you'll find those valuable. With that, I wish you the best on your journey to mastering yourself and fulfilling your purpose/calling. Hopefully, I will get to experience the light of your identity and purpose as it shines around the world.

You're capable of amazing things and the time to start doing those amazing things is NOW. LET'S GO!! (Godspeed!!)

"Inaction breeds doubt and fear. Action breeds confidence and courage. If you want to conquer fear, do not sit home and think about it. Go out and get busy." —Dale Carnegie

Acknowledgement

A BIG "Thank you" to everyone who supported me in this book project. Those who were kind enough to complete the survey about the book; those who gave feedback about the book; those who helped with reviewing and editing the book. I really appreciate you all. Also, to the readers, I extend gratitude to you as well for your trust and your time. I hope you found this book helpful in the area of your identity. I will definitely love to hear from you.(I am open to feedback.)

References

Introduction

[1] Christoph Schimmele, Jonathan Fonberg and Grant Schellenberg (March 24, 2021). *Canadians' assessments of social media in their lives* . Retrieved March 29th, 2022 from https://www150.statcan.gc.ca/n1/pub/36-28-0001/2021003/article/00004-eng.htm

Chapter 3

[1] Todd Herman. (May 1, 2019). *Why Every Entrepreneur Needs to Know About the 'Alter Ego Effect'*. Retrieved February 20, 2022 from https://www.entrepreneur.com/article/333074

[2] Courtney E. Ackerman, MA. (Updated March 28, 2022). *What is Self-Acceptance? 25 Exercises + Definition and Quotes*. Retrieved February 21, 2022 from https://positivepsychology.com/self-acceptance/

[3] Sarah-Len Mutiwasekwa. (November 12, 2019). *Self-love*. Retrieved February 25, 2022 from https://www.psychologytoday.com/ca/blog/the-upside-things/201911/self-love

[4] Toni Bernhard J.D. (April 2, 2019). *How to Turn Harmful Self-Talk Into Helpful Self-Talk*. Retrieved February 26, 2022 from https:// www.psychologytoday.com/ca/blog/turning-straw-gold/201904/how-turn-harmful-self-talk-helpful-self-talk

[5] Psychology Today. *Inner Voice*. Retrieved February 26, 2022 from https://www.psychologytoday.com/ca/basics/self-talk

Chapter 4

[1] Psychology iResearchNet. *Self-Affirmation Theory*. Retrieved March 6, 2022 from http:// psychology.iresearchnet.com/social-psychology/social-psychology-theories/self-affirmation-theory/

[2] Catherine Moore, Psychologist, MBA. (Updated March 24, 2022). *Positive Daily Affirmations: Is There Science Behind It?*. Retrieved March 3, 2022 from https://positivepsychology.com/daily-affirmations/

Chapter 5

[1] Dr. Saul McLeod. (2018). (2018). *Erik Erikson's Stages of Psychosocial Development*. Retrieved March 12, 2022 from https://www.simplypsychology.org/Erik-Erikson.html

Resources

1. Color Code Personality test : https://www.colorcode.com/choose_personality_test/
2. Enneagram personality test: https://www.truity.com/test/enneagram-personality-test
3. The 16 personalities test: https://www.16personalities.com/free-personality-test
4. Core values list: https://scottjeffrey.com/core-values-list/
5. Courage and Self-esteem - Earl Nightingale: https://www.youtube.com/watch?v=dTeIgDjAGp0
6. S.H.A.P.E Assessment, DayBreak Academy: https://daybreak-academy.org/wp-content/uploads/2017/03/S.H.A.P.E-Assessment-DA.pdf
7. SHAPED to make a difference: https://pastorrick.com/series/shaped-to-make-a-difference/

Recommended reading

1. The Identity Shift: Upgrade How You Operate To Elevate Your Life by Anthony Trucks
2. Six pillars of self-esteem: The Definitive Work on Self-Esteem by the Leading Pioneer in the Field by Nathaniel Branden
3. Shaken: Discovering Your True Identity In The Midst of Life's Storm by Tim Tebow

4. The Purpose-driven Life: What on Earth Am I
Here For? by Rick Warren

Thank you in advance

If indeed you found value in this book, I would really appreciate it if you would kindly leave a review on the book page on Amazon (I like 5 stars!) That'll mean the world to me.

Other book(s) by author

- Be A High Achiever: Achieving All-round Success In College & University

- Crack The Dream Job Code: How To Land Your Dream Job In Canada As An Immigrant

ABOUT FRANKLIN

Franklin H. Ezenwa is an author, speaker and IT professional. He is also the author of 2 Amazon bestselling books. Being very passionate about helping people to achieve their goals and being the best version of themselves, Franklin shares valuable insights

through speaking and writing. He's also enthusiastic about working with people, having had opportunities to mentor others in both school and workplace environments. Franklin has served in leadership roles in various settings and has had the privilege of speaking to different groups.

https://allroundachievers.com

Special _FREE_ Bonus Gift for you

To help you achieve more success with this book, there are
FREE BONUS RESOURCES for you at :

rebrand.ly/FreeGiftIdentity

- Identity Manual Workbook
- Printables with powerful affirmations for a formidable identity
- Empowering quotes eBook